Cair
Lilith's Daughter

By Walter Parks
Paperback Edition
Copyright 2012
UnKnownTruths
Publishing Company

UnKnownTruths
Publishing Company
8815 Conroy Windermere Rd. Ste 190
Orlando, FL 32835

My Blog

My Website

Other titles by Walter Parks for Kindle:

Jesus the Missing Years

Atlantis the Eyewitnesses

Immortal Again

Aging is a Treatable Disease

Paranormal Portal to a Parallel Universe

Alligator Attack!

The Devil Takes the Bodies

Contents

Preface

One of the enduring questions concerning the accuracy of the Bible is the question: who was Cain's wife.

Most true believers in the validity of the Bible speculate that she was a descendent of Adam and Eve; that she was a sister or cousin of Cain.

Others believe that she was some sort of pre-human; an earlier product of evolution just before Cain was born.

Who she was is a troubling question for believers and even for most non-believers because many such were taught and grew up in the traditional religious beliefs.

I grew up in the Southern Baptist tradition but my career has been in the scientifically based aerospace industry.

I had to search to find who Can's wife could have been.

I tried to stick to the words in the Bible.

I augmented those words with words from original parts of the Bible before they were so drastically modified in the late BC time periods and the early AD time periods.

I was also forced to use my own speculations to fill in the missing gaps of information.

I hope you find my attempt in answering the enduring question to be at least somewhat informative.

I hope you enjoy.

Introduction

Cain had an urge that he could not suppress. He had it before, but now it was so compelling that he had to do something about it.

Hormones were surging through his young body creating a hunger beyond his control.

He knew that his parents, even though they were mad at him would not want him to go, but he had to go and to go now!

He edged through the brush and looked back at his parents. They were lying on the ground under the apple tree admiring its ripening fruit.

He left his home in the garden and went east into the land of Nod, the land of the wanderer.

He went searching to fulfill his urge.

After hours of searching he saw Lilim. He knew immediately that she was what he was searching for. She was the most exotic creature that he had ever seen.

She should be; she was the daughter of the renowned Lilith!

She was young and had just reached her maturity. Her long black hair reached down below her tiny waist. Her eyes were much larger than he had ever seen, and they sparkled!

Her breasts were large for her youth and her wide hips proved that she was now a woman.

She stared back at him in wonder. She had never seen a human.

He continued to stare in awe. She dropped her arms so he could better see her. She smiled.

He wondered; what did that mean?

She stood standing still with her arms out to her side for a long moment.

He took a step towards her and stopped.

She continued to stand as still as a statue.

The hormones surged through his body and prepared him to fulfill his urge.

She looked down at the results of his hormone surge, then back to his face and smiled again.

He stared into those very large eyes and the curves of her over sized breasts and hips and the tiny waist in between. He wasn't sure what to do.

He could not stop a throbbing in his groins that quickly took over his entire body.

He started to quickly move towards her but he was not quick enough. His seed started erupting on the ground.

She laughed.

He grabbed her and followed through with what his hormones demanded.

This event was later summarized in the Bible:

"Then Cain went away from the presence of the Lord (the Garden of Eden) and settled in the land of Nod, east of Eden. Cain knew his wife...." Genesis 4:16-17

Let's learn more about Cain and this exotic creature.

Chapter 1
Cain

Cain was the first human born on planet earth. This is a true statement regardless of your religious beliefs.

If you believe the Bible, Cain was the first born human because his parents were not born but created by God.

If you are a non-believer in the Bible and believe in evolution you know that there had to be a first human; Cain is as good a name for him as any other.

So by all beliefs, Cain was the first born human.

But there were thousands of pre-humans before Cain and some of them also lived at the same time as Cain. This cannot be disputed because of the enormous amounts of fossils that they left behind.

Let's examine the undisputable facts that the fossils prove.

We humans are in life's scientific classification called genus Homo.

Fossil evidence places the beginning of the genus Homo at two million years ago with the emergence of Homo habilis from East and Southern Africa.

This species is the earliest fossil record of man-like creatures that is categorized in the same group as living humans. It was at this point in time that stone tools first appeared and near human-like activities began.

Homo habilis represents a major change from other earlier species of primitive forms of humans. Up to this point in time of 2 million years ago, Africa is the only location in the world where fossils have been found for human-like existence.

At 1.75 million years ago, Homo erectus (a.k.a. Homo ergaster) appears and spreads throughout North Africa eventually traveling to Eurasia. Homo erectus and close variants including Homo ergaster and Homo heidelbergensis survived for 1.5 million years in Africa and Asia.

They were active hunters that lived in small huts and caves, mastered the use of fire and fashioned a variety of stone tools.

But there was a related genus before the Homo genus appearance 2 million years ago.

Australopithecus Afarensis

Fossils show that Australopithecus Afarensis was a pre-human that lived between 3.9 and 2.9 million years ago. It was more closely related to our genus Homo than any other known primate from the same time period. There is not enough evidence to determine whether Australopithecus Afarensis was a direct ancestor or a close relative of an unknown ancestor.

The most famous Australopithecus Afarensis fossil is the partial skeleton named Lucy which was found to be 3.2 million years old. Illustrations of how she may have looked and lived were made.

Australopithecus Afarensis

Some Australopithecus Afarensis left human-like footprints on volcanic ash in Laetoli, Kenya.

It is believed by some that Australopithecus Afarensis was an ancestral to both the genus Australopithecus and the genus Homo.

Compared to the modern and extinct great apes, Australopithecus Afarensis had reduced canines and molars, although they were still relatively larger than in modern humans.

Australopithecus Afarensis also has a relatively small brain size and a projecting face as compared to modern humans.

Australopithecus Afarensis fossils have been found in Savannah environments and likely increased its diet to include meat from scavenging opportunities.

Back to Homo erectus

Fully developed Homo erectus fossils have been found in Northern Africa and China from about 500,000 years ago.

From 500,000 years ago to 250,000 years ago, Homo erectus was transitioning into an archaic form of Homo sapiens in Africa and Europe.

The most famous variety of archaic Homo sapiens is undoubtedly the Neanderthal people. Scientists classify them as a sub-species of Homo sapiens: Homo sapiens neanderthalensis. With the emergence of Neanderthals comes a new, more advanced and specialized tool technology called the Mousterian Tradition.

We see signs of developing Neanderthals arising about 300,000 years ago. They populated regions in

Europe and the Near East and existed right up to just 28,000 years ago in western France.

Current evidence shows that despite Neanderthals' stockier build, they share several key features with modern man. There is also clear evidence that they had control of fire, lived in caves or open-air structures of stone and vegetation.

Homo habilis

Homo habilis is thought to be the ancestor of the lankier and more sophisticated Homo ergaster and lived side by side with early Homo erectus until at least 1.44 million years ago.

Homo habilis

Back to Homo erectus

Later Day Homo erectus Illustrated

Homo erectus hunted with tools.

Homo erectus family

This diorama in the National Museum of Indonesia, Jakarta, depicts the life size model of a Homo erectus family living on the island of Java in Indonesia about 900,000 years ago.

Several different but closely related species also lived between 1.8 million and 1.3 million years ago.

We Homo sapiens first reached anatomical modernity about 200,000 years ago and began to exhibit full behavioral modernity around 50,000 years ago.

Homo erectus would bear a striking resemblance to modern humans, but had a brain about 74 percent of the size of modern man. Its forehead is less sloping and the teeth are smaller.

Other hominid designations such as Homo georgicus, Homo ergaster, Homo pekinensis, and Homo heidelbergensis are often put under the umbrella species name of Homo erectus.

Starting with Homo georgicus found in what is now the Republic of Georgia dated at 1.8 million years ago, the pelvis and backbone grew more human-like and gave Homo georgicus the ability to cover very long distances in order to follow herds of other animals. This is the oldest fossil of a hominid found (so far) outside of Africa.

Control of fire by early archaic humans was achieved 1.5 million years ago by Homo ergaster. Homo ergaster reached a height of about 6.2 feet.

Evolution of dark skin, which is linked to the loss of body hair in human ancestors, is complete by 1.2 million years ago. Homo pekinensis first appears in Asia around 700 thousand years ago but according to the theory of a recent African origin of modern humans, they could not be human ancestors, but rather, were just a cousin offshoot species from Homo ergaster.

Homo heidelbergensis was a very large hominid that had a more advanced complement of cutting tools and may have hunted big game such as horses.

Homo antecessor may be a common ancestor of humans and Neanderthals.

Homo antecessor is an extinct human species (or subspecies) dating from 1.2 million to 800,000 years ago and is one of the earliest known archaic human varieties in Europe.

Some believe that Homo antecessor was a separate species that evolved from Homo ergaster and inhabited Europe from 600,000 to 250,000 years ago.

Humans have approximately 20,000–25,000 genes and share 99% of their DNA with the now extinct

Neanderthal and 95-99% of their DNA with their closest living evolutionary relative, the chimpanzees.

The human variant of the FOXP2 gene (linked to the control of speech) has been found to be identical in Neanderthals. It can therefore be deduced that Homo antecessor would also have had the human FOXP2 gene.

A reconstruction of Homo heidelbergensis suggests how he may have looked.

Homo heidelbergensis

Homo heidelbergensis was about 5 feet tall. He left footprints in powdery volcanic ash solidified in Italy. Homo heidelbergensis is believed to be a common ancestor of humans and Neanderthals. He is morphologically very similar to Homo erectus but Homo heidelbergensis had a larger brain-case, about 93% the size of that of us Homo sapiens.

Homo heidelbergensis, often called "Heidelberg Man" was named after the University of Heidelberg. His stone tool technology was very close to that used by Homo erectus.

Recent findings in a pit in Atapuerca (Spain) of 28 skeletons suggest that Homo heidelbergensis may have been the first species of the Homo genus to bury their dead.

Some experts believe that Homo heidelbergensis, like its descendant Homo neanderthalensis, acquired a primitive form of language. No forms of art or sophisticated artifacts other than stone tools have been uncovered, although red ochre, a mineral that can be used to create a red pigment which is useful as a paint, has been found at Terra Amata excavations in the south of France.

The morphology of the outer and middle ear suggests they had an auditory sensitivity similar to modern humans and very different from chimpanzees. They were probably able to differentiate between many different sounds. Dental wear analysis suggests they were as likely to be right-handed as modern people.

Homo heidelbergensis was a close relative (most probably a migratory descendant) of Homo ergaster. Homo ergaster is thought to be the first hominine to vocalize and that as Homo heidelbergensis developed more sophisticated culture proceeded from this point.

Sufficiently accurate dated fossils prove beyond any doubt that many varieties of archaic humans lived before Cain and some of them lived at the same time as Cain.

Cain was the first born of Homo sapiens, a true human. He was born in about 200,000 BC.

Chapter 2
Following the DNA

DNA is God's, or if you are a non-believer, Mother Nature's primary tool of creating Man and all life forms on planet earth.

After creating the first Hominoid about 6 million years age, a minor change was made in its DNA to create the next species. This process continued until about 2 million years ago when the genus Homo was established.

The process then continued until 200,000 years ago when Homo sapiens came to be and Cain was born. The process is still continuing today.

The genetic difference between individual humans today averages a minuscule 0.1% (.001). It is only 1.2% between humans and the chimpanzee.

The DNA difference between us and gorillas is about 1.6%. Most importantly, chimpanzees, bonobos, and humans all show this same amount of difference from gorillas.

A difference of 3.1% distinguishes us "African apes" from the Asian great ape, the orangutan.

All of the great apes and humans differ from the rhesus monkeys, for example, by about 7% in their DNA.

The DNA evidence shows that our human creation/evolutionary tree is embedded within the great apes tree. In the scientific classifications we are classified as a great ape.

Don't get upset; it's just the name of a classification.

The fossil evidence supports this DNA evidence, or should I say that this DNA evidence supports the fossil evidence.

Let's summarize.

Due to billions of years of creation/evolution, humans share genes with all living organisms, including plants. The percentage of genes or DNA that organisms share records their similarities. We share more genes with organisms that are more closely related to us.

We have already discussed the very high percentages of DNA that we share with the apes. But we also share high percentages of our DNA with all living creatures. We share 90% with cats, 80% with cows, 75% with mice, 60% with the fruit fly, and 50% with the banana.

Yes, the banana!

Animal and plant life share so much ancient DNA coding because animals and plants had the same ancestors way back and did not diverge until approximately 1.5 billion years ago.

Humans belong to the biological group known as Primates, and are classified with the great apes, one of the major groups of the primate creation/evolutionary tree. Besides similarities in anatomy and behavior, our close biological kinship with other primate species is indicated by DNA evidence. It confirms that our closest living biological relatives are chimpanzees and bonobos, with whom we share many traits.

But we did not evolve directly from any primates living today.

DNA shows that our species and chimpanzees diverged from a common ancestor species that lived between 8 and 6 million years ago. The last common ancestor of monkeys and apes lived about 25 million years ago.

Chapter 3
The Garden of Eden

The Bible and other evidence suggest that Cain was born in a garden like paradise where food was plentiful. The Bible called it the Garden of Eden.

The Bible tells us the following about the location of Eden.

And the LORD God planted a garden eastward in Eden; and there he put the man whom he had formed. Genesis 2:8

And out of the ground made the LORD God to grow every tree that is pleasant to the sight, and good for food; the tree of life also in the midst of the garden, and the tree of knowledge of good and evil. Genesis 2:9

And a river went out of Eden to water the garden; and from thence it was parted, and became into four heads. Genesis 2:10

The name of the first is Pison: that is it which compasseth the whole land of Havilah, where there is gold; Genesis 2:11

And the gold of that land is good: there is bdellium and the onyx stone. Genesis 2:12

And the name of the second river is Gihon: the same is it that compasseth the whole land of Ethiopia. Genesis 2:13

And the name of the third river is Hiddekel: that is it which goeth toward the east of Assyria. And the fourth river is Euphrates. Genesis 2:14

The Bible is telling us that Eden was located between the Euphrates and Hiddekel rivers. The

Hiddekel River is believed to be the Tigris River in Iraq.

And the LORD God took the man, and put him into the Garden of Eden to dress it and to keep it. Genesis 2:15

So we are told that Eden was somewhere between the Euphrates and Tigris Rivers. But where are the Pison and Gihon Rivers?

The area of where they and the Garden of Eden existed has changed dramatically over the 200,000 years since Cain left the Garden of Eden.

The area has been subjected to volcanoes and plate tectonics during all this very long time.

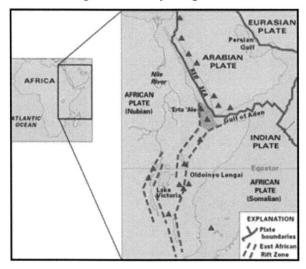

The Map of East Africa shows some of the historically active volcanoes (red triangles) and the Afar Triangle (shaded, center) which is a triple junction where three plates are pulling away from one another: the Arabian Plate, and the two parts of the African Plate (the Nubian Plate and the Somali Plate) splitting along the East African Rift Zone.

Scientists have been tracking this activity by satellite and can clearly see the Arabian tectonic plate and the African plate still moving away from each other, stretching the Earth's crust and widening the southern end of the Red Sea.

This activity is accompanied by a large series of earthquakes along a 37-mile section of the East African Rift in Afar, Ethiopia.

Over a period of three weeks, the crust on the sides of the rift moved apart by 26 feet and magma (molten rock), enough to fill a football stadium more than 2,000 times was injected along a vertical crack, forming a new crust.

Similar activity at this location has been going on for the past 30 million years forming the 186-mile wide Afar depression.

So the area was very different when Cain was born.

I should also point out that silts and various settlements that flowed down the drainage basin of this area made continuous deposits in the river beds and caused the rivers to change course many times. Research in the area shows that the Euphrates River moved west several times and that the Tigers moved east at least once in the last 4,000 years.

You can imagine how much movement occurred over the 200,000 years since Cain's birth!

Nevertheless the clues from the Bible point us to the location of the Garden of Eden.

Two of the 4 rivers describing the location of the Garden of Eden still exist in approximately their old locations.

The Pison and Gihon however have dried up as the climate became much dryer and their beds filled with sediments. Tectonic plate activity and Noah's Flood also changed the land.

Satellite photos show many dried up beds that could be the ancient rivers.

Let's take a look at the 2 remaining rivers, the Euphrates and the Tigris to try to locate the Garden of Eden.

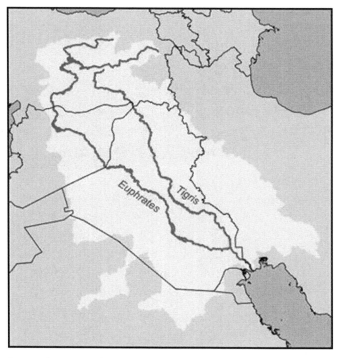

It can be speculated that the Pison and the Gihon Rivers flowed into the Euphrates or the Tigris Rivers north of the point where the map shows their close approach. Further the Euphrates and Tigris rivers could then have merged at the point that shows their close approach. This would result in one river as described in the Bible. Genesis 2:10. Let's call it the Eden River.

Perhaps south of this merged point the Euphrates and Tigris Rivers may or may not have forked off this Eden River and then merged again before flowing into the Persian Gulf.

The Bible and the evidence tell us that the Garden of Eden was in current day Iraq south of Bagdad and near the top of the Persian Gulf into which both the Euphrates and Tigris Rivers flow.

The current topography may best be visualized by a modern map of the area.

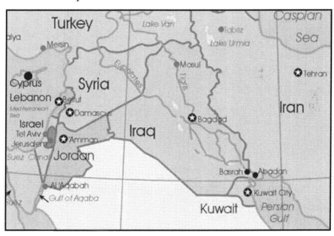

It therefore can be assumed that Eden was located
just south of the ancient merger points of the
Euphrates and Tigris Rivers. The Garden of Eden
would then likely be in the fertile south part of
Eden. Some argue that the Garden of Eden may
actually be under water at the top of the Persian
Gulf because this area was flooded.

So the Biblical evidence tells us that Cain was born
in what is current day Iraq between the current
positions of the Euphrates and Tigris Rivers.

**But scientists have told us that mankind first
appeared in Africa.**

So which is correct; Africa or Iraq?

It has long been believed that the first true humans
originated in Africa about 200,000 years ago and
did not migrate out of Africa until about 70,000
years ago.

But the Bible tells us that the first man, Adam and his family were in the Garden of Eden by the Euphrates River which is in Iraq.

Now recently 400,000 year old human (or near human) teeth have been found in a cave in Israel.

This supports that "near humans", perhaps Homo erectus, were in the Iraq area about 400,000 and certainly by 200,000 years ago.

Therefore the sequence previously described leading to Cain's birth is most likely correct.

Cain was indeed the first born of Homo sapiens and he was born in about 200,000 BC in the Garden of Eden in what is now Iraq.

Chapter 4
Lilith

Lilith is mentioned throughout the ancient literature, primarily as an extremely exotic and seductive woman.

The Bible, before it was later changed to the current Bible tells us that she was a mate of the first human, Adam, before Eve arrived.

But she was not human. She was among the latest of the Homo erectus species. But she looked almost human.

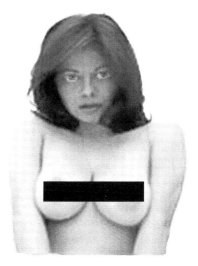

The current Bible only mentions her one time, in Isaiah 34:14:

Wildcats shall meet with hyenas, goat-demons shall call to each other; there too Lilith shall repose, and find a place to rest.

The writer of Isaiah grouped her with the animals; perhaps primarily because she was not human;

perhaps because of her earlier relationship with Adam: and maybe because she was so seductive.

Isaiah is primarily focused on the oncoming judgment of the Lord. The animals listed before Lilith as well as Lilith herself are said to inherit a desolate Earth after divine judgment. Lilith is cast out of the holy land and the grace of God, a clear sign of rejection; because she was not human or because she first "knew" Adam?

There was obviously some sort of mythology behind Lilith when Isaiah was written, but what that story is has been omitted from the current Bible. Perhaps the writer assumed the audience knew the story of Lilith and there was no need for elaboration. What we can glean from this mention though is that she was viewed as a negative figure from a very early point

We may get better insight from the Alphabet of Jesus ben Sirach (Alphabetum Siracidis, Othijoth ben Sira) which is attributed to the author of the Wisdom of Sirach.

The Wisdom of Sirach or simply Sirach, and also known as The Book Ecclesiasticus or Siracides is a work from the early 2nd century B.C. (approximately 200-175 B.C.) written by the Jewish scribe Jesus ben Sirach of Jerusalem.

This book was not accepted into the Hebrew Bible and as a result the original Hebrew text was not preserved in the Jewish canon. However, various original Hebrew versions have since been recovered.

There are numerous citations of Sirach in the Talmud and works of rabbinic literature.

Despite not finding ultimate acceptance into the scriptural canon of Judaism, it was read as scripture by some Jews. For instance, it was included in the canon of the Jewish Septuagint, the 2nd century BC Greek version of the Jewish scriptures which were widely used.

Sirach is also accepted as part of the Christian Biblical canon by Catholics, Eastern Orthodox, and most Oriental Orthodox but not by most Protestants.

The Latin Church Fathers termed it Ecclesiasticus because it was frequently read in churches, leading to the title liber ecclesiasticus which is Latin and Greek for "church book".

It is dated to anywhere between A.D. 700 and 1000. It is a compilation of proverbs with commentary. The work contains references to masturbation, incest and flatulence.

The main section of interest here is titled Lilith and is best known because of its reference to Lilith:

While God created Adam, who was alone, He said, 'It is not good for man to be alone'. He also created a woman, from the earth, as He had created Adam himself, and called her Lilith.

This section of the old Bible was revised and now the current Bible reads:

And God said, Let us make man in our image, after our likeness: and let them have dominion over the fish of the sea, and over the fowl of the air, and over the cattle, and over all the earth, and over every creeping thing that creepeth upon the earth. Genesis 1:26

So God created man in his own image, in the image of God created he him; male and female created he them. Genesis 1:27

This Bible verse describes the creation of Adam and Lilith in the same manner. You will remember that the second version of creation, also in Genesis as shown below, God created Eve from Adam's rib.

So apparently Lilith was Adam's mate before the arrival of the first true human woman, Eve. Note that Lilith was not created in "**….in our image, after our likeness….**" Lilith was not a true human but of the Homo erectus species.

Adam and Lilith did not get along and Lilith left Adam and the Garden.

God sent three angels to bring her back but she did not come back.

So God created another mate for Adam as described below:

And the LORD God said, it is not good that the man should be alone; I will make him a help mate. Genesis 2:18

And the LORD God caused a deep sleep to fall upon Adam, and he slept: and he took one of his ribs, and closed up the flesh instead thereof; Genesis 2:21

And the rib, which the LORD God had taken from man, made he a woman, and brought her unto the man. Genesis 2:22

And Adam called his wife's name Eve, because she was the mother of all living. Genesis 3:20

And so God gave Adam another wife, a totally human wife, Eve, who he created directly from Adam.

Back to Lilith

Lilith left the Garden and went into the wilderness where her kind (Homo erectus) dwelt.

There are many stories in the ancient Jewish literature of what Lilith did after leaving the Garden.

One such story has Lilith mating with Samael who later became the angel of death. This is covered in a forth coming book:

The Sons of God
The Daughters of Men

Most of the many legends of Lilith have bad connotations of her. But the story of her exotic sexual nature has been the most enduring.

In the Christian Middle Ages Lilith and her daughter Lilim became the personification of licentiousness and lust. They became identified with succubae who would copulate with men in their sleep, causing them to have nocturnal emissions or "wet dreams."

Lilith therefore became known as the primary succubus.

Through the literature of the Kabbalah, Lilith became fixed in Jewish demonology where her primary role is that of a seducer of men. The Kabbalah further enhanced her demonic character by making her the partner of Samael (i.e. Satan) and queen of the realm of the forces of evil.

If you ask how Lilith herself, the first wife of Adam became evil, the answer lies in her insubordination to her husband Adam. It is her independence from Adam, her position beyond the control of a male that makes her "evil."

She is disobedient and like all women who are willful, she is perceived as posing a constant threat to the divinely ordered state of affairs defined and controlled by men.

Lilith is represented as a powerfully sexual woman against whom men had no defenses. Lilith is the personification of female sexuality.

In her demonized form, Lilith is a frightening and threatening creature who personifies the real sexual power women exercise over men.

She represents the deeper, darker fear men have of women and female sexuality. This is why female sexuality, as a result of this fear, has been repressed and subjected to the severest controls in Western patriarchal society. And so too has the figure of Lilith been kept hidden.

However, she lurks as a powerful unidentified presence, an unspoken name, in the minds of Biblical commentators who identify women as the true source of evil in the world. It wasn't just eating the apple; it was primarily her sexual control over men.

In the Apocryphal Testament of Reuben (one of the Testaments of the Twelve Patriarchs, ostensibly the twelve sons of Jacob), for example, it is explained that:

Women are evil, my children: because they have no power or strength to stand up against man, they use wiles and try to ensnare him by their charms; and man, whom woman cannot subdue by strength, she subdues by guile. Testament of Reuben: V, 1-2, 5

References to Lilith in the Talmud describe her as a night demon with long hair. Crudely drawn images of Lilith can be seen on ancient amulets and incantation bowls.

Despite the fact that she is not officially recognized in the Christian tradition, in the Late Middle Ages she is occasionally identified with the serpent in Genesis 3 and shown accordingly with a woman's head and torso. For example, the bare-breasted woman with a snake's lower parts posed seductively with Adam and Eve in ancient depictions.

There is considerable evidence from ancient literature, including books thrown out of the original Bible that Lilith was Adam's first mate. She was systematically removed from Christian literature. But her shadow remains as the personification of an exotic, sexually powerful woman that still inhabits the minds of men. The deep seated genetic memory of her may well be a cause of the wet dreams of men.

Chapter 5
Lilim, Daughter of Lilith

Even though the story of Lilith disappeared from the canonical Bible, her daughter Lilim haunted men for over a thousand years. It was well into the Middle Ages that Jews still manufactured amulets to keep away Lilim. Supposedly she was a lusty she-demon who copulated with men in all their dreams, causing nocturnal emissions.

Greeks adopted the belief of the Lilim. Christians adopted the belief, calling her a harlot of hell, or succubus.

Even though most of the Lilith and Lilim legends are derived from Jewish folklore, descriptions of the Lilith and Lilim demons appear in Iranian, Babylonian, Mexican, Greek, Arab, English, German, Oriental and Native American legends. In medieval Europe she was proclaimed to be the wife, concubine or grandmother of Satan.

According to Jewish folklore and Kabbalistic teachings Lilith was believed to be the sexual, pleasurable manifestation of the Goddess or the prime deity of the prevailing religion which ancient Judaism sought to destroy.

Such folklore said Lilith and Lilim had control of life or death over any child produced by any sexual union not prescribed by Jewish law including husband and wife in candle light, the woman completely naked, or at a time forbidden by the law.

Children engendered under such conditions were referred to as oppressed souls. According to Jewish law the sexual union must be kept sacred, any act or omission rendering it less placed the child engendered under the power of Lilith.

Such Jewish law was strictly anti-natural as can be seen. For example, if the husband lusted for his wife's naked body, or committed any forbidden sexual act he was said to have permitted Lilith to enter the impregnated womb and therefore have power over the child. It goes without saying that any child conceived out of wedlock was thought to be a child of Lilith, or Lilim, because bastards could not be lawfully conceived.

Today many would call such laws ridiculous and inhumane, but remember these were Jewish religious laws placed upon people chosen by God who were to obey him in their every act of life. It was universally believed even until the last century that any strong thought or emotion in the minds of a man or woman during lovemaking would impress itself on the engendered fetus.

For example, it was superstitiously thought if a dog barking frightened the woman at the moment of climax the produced child would have hair growing all over its face. If either parent grimaced in pleasure during lovemaking, a child born of the union would have ugly or twisted facial features.

Such regulations were to completely destroy all lustful and sexual pleasure between husband and wife and make their sexual union strictly for propagation. At times the regulations were not solely for prohibitive purposes. It should be noted that love and romance were not introduced to general society until the eleventh and thirteenth centuries by the troubadours in southern France and then spread to Italy and to the Mediterranean.

Many marriages of nobility were prearranged and sanctified by the Church and involved retaining and expending territory. This is why the male often had a mistress.

Of course Christianity had its regulations too, for example, the Catholic Church frequently counseled good Catholics to make love under the portrait of Jesus or the Virgin Mary, and to keep religious thoughts in their minds during their mutual climax (believed necessary for the mingling of the male and female "sperms"). Failure to do this could result in their child receiving some physical imperfection because of their sin as well as falling under the influence of the Devil.

There is a saying that Catholics are influenced by the Church from the cradle to the grave, but the previous counseling makes it pre-cradle.

As one can see most of these regulations, no matter under what circumstance, were obviously to detach the engendering of children from the natural life process. Regulations had to be followed so that the influence of evil could be avoided.

It is no wonder Lilith and Lilim survived so long; they served a double purpose, frighten the people into religious servitude and strengthen the power of the religious leaders.

Lilim was so sexually erotic that she could not be refused; Cain had to have her.

Chapter 6
Life with Lilim

Cain made love to his wife and she became pregnant and gave birth to Enoch. Cain was then building a city and he named it after his son Enoch. Genesis 4:17, 18

This is the Bible's first mention of a city.

Apparently Cain and his family and associates built some sort of walled enclosure about the place where they dwelt. The definition of a city in that early time literally meant enclosure.

Cain's associates were initially Homo erectus "people" that dwelt in the land of Nod.

Cain built the city in the land of Nod, east of the Garden of Eden in about 200,000 BC.

The previous mentioned plate tectonics, volcanoes, and river sediments completely changed the area down through the ages.

Noah's Flood occurred in 9619 BC (See the book **Noah's Flood, When Where Why**) and made even more significant changes.

We have seen from the previous chapters that Eden was located between the Tigris and Euphrates Rivers in the present-day Middle Eastern country of Iraq. The ancients named this area Mesopotamia, which means "the land between the rivers" or "the land between two rivers."

In ancient times the city of UR was the capital city of Mesopotamia. Its ruins are between the modern city of Baghdad, Iraq, and the head of the Persian Gulf.

Ur was the home of the Biblical patriarch Abraham who was a prophet through whom numerous major world religions trace their early origins.

Cain's city of Enoch was located towards the east of this area. It can be speculated that after Enoch was destroyed by Noah's Flood that it was rebuilt on the banks of the Euphrates River at the place where the River was located after the Flood.

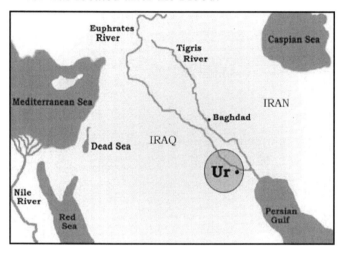

The Bible and ancient documents indicate that Cain and Lilim had many children and a long line of descendents.

The Bible and ancient documents also indicate that Cain and his descendents were always thought less of than the other descendents of Adam and Eve. This could be because Cain had killed his brother, but it may be because his early descendents were not true humans but half-breeds, between the human Cain and the Homo erectus Lilim.

But all indications are that they survived and successfully added to the growing "human" population of planet earth.

Epilog

The enduring question has been: "Where did Cain get his wife?"

The churches have not given an acceptable answer to this question. Their inability to answer this question creates great doubt as to the accuracy of the Bible. More and more Christians are giving up on defending the Bible.

It is vitally important for Christians to be able to answer this question because it relates to defending the fact that all humans are descendants of Adam and Eve and only their descendants can be saved.

Cain's wife was a major discussion at the famous Scopes (Monkey) Trial and the film made about it, "Inherit the Wind".

Cain's wife has been talked about in countries all over the world for hundreds of years.

Skeptics of the Bible have used Cain's wife time and again to try to discredit the book of Genesis as a true historical record.

At the historic Scopes Trial in Tennessee in 1925, William Jennings Bryan, the prosecutor who stood for the Christian faith, failed to answer the question about Cain's wife posed by the ACLU lawyer Clarence Darrow. Consider the following excerpt from the trial record as Darrow interrogates Bryan:

Q—Did you ever discover where Cain got his wife?

A—No, sir; I leave the agnostics to hunt for her.

Q—You have never found out?

A—I have never tried to find.

Q—You have never tried to find?

A—No.

Q—The Bible says he got one doesn't it? Were there other people on the earth at that time?

A—I cannot say.

Q—You cannot say. Did that ever enter your consideration?

A—Never bothered me.

Q—There were no others recorded, but Cain got a wife.

A—That is what the Bible says.

Q—Where she came from you do not know?

The world's press was focused on this trial, and what they heard still affects Christianity to this day; Christians still cannot defend the Biblical record of how Cain got a wife.

Why Is It Important?

It is important because it forces us to formulate an answer to the question and in so doing we see the way to reconcile the Bible with the scientific facts of creation/evolution.

These creation/evolutionary facts cannot be disputed because that are proven by the abundance of fossils of lives that came before us and because the DNA of all life have relations that prove the chain of creation/evolution.

We and all animals and plants, all life, came from the same ancestor. We continue to have the genes created/evolved in this process. We are related to all life on earth.

DNA is God's, or if you are a non-believer, Mother Nature's primary tool of creating Man and all life forms on planet earth.

After creating the first Hominoid about 6 million years age, a minor change was made in its DNA to create the next species.

The genetic difference between individual humans today averages a minuscule 0.1% (.001). It is only 1.2% between humans and the chimpanzee.

The DNA difference between us and gorillas is about 1.6%. Most importantly, chimpanzees, bonobos, and humans all show this same amount of difference from gorillas.

A difference of 3.1% distinguishes us "African apes" from the Asian great ape, the orangutan.

All of the great apes and humans differ from the rhesus monkeys, for example, by about 7% in their DNA.

The DNA evidence shows that the human creation/evolutionary tree is embedded within the great apes tree. In the scientific classifications we are classified as a great ape.

The fossil evidence supports this DNA evidence, or should I say that this DNA evidence supports the fossil evidence.

Let's summarize.

Due to billions of years of creation/evolution, humans share genes with all living organisms, including plants. The percentage of genes or DNA that organisms share records their similarities. We share more genes with organisms that are more closely related to us.

We have already discussed the very high percentages of DNA that we share with the apes. But we also share high percentages of our DNA with all living creatures. We share 90% with cats, 80% with cows, 75% with mice, 60% with the fruit fly, and 50% with the banana.

Yes, the banana!

Animal and plant life share so much ancient DNA coding because animals and plants had the same ancestors way back and did not diverged until approximately1.5 billion years ago.

Humans belong to the biological group known as Primates, and are classified with the great apes, one of the major groups of the primate creation/evolutionary tree. Besides similarities in anatomy and behavior, our close biological kinship with other primate species is indicated by DNA evidence. It confirms that our closest living biological relatives are chimpanzees and bonobos, with whom we share many traits. But we did not evolve nor were we created directly from any primates living today.

DNA shows that our species and chimpanzees diverged from a common ancestor species that lived between 8 and 6 million years ago. The last common ancestor of monkeys and apes lived about 25 million years ago.

There came a time when the first human man appeared. The Bible named him Adam.

The Bible then describes the creation of 2 women for him. The first was Lilith (Genesis 1:27) but her name was removed from the current Bible. However her name can be seen in the older version of the Bible that existed before later day changes were made.

The creation of Eve, Adam's second mate, was created from Adam's rib and is described in Genesis 2:18.

Lilith has been systematically removed from the Bible, except for one reference in Isaiah 34:14.

Not only was Lilith removed from the Bible, but she was demonized.

The facts remain that she did exist and she did have children that are mentioned throughout the ancient literature. At lease one of her daughters was called Lilim.

This story of Cain's wife is my initial attempt to reconcile the Bible with the undisputable scientific evidence for creative evolution. I have combined 4 sets of information: The current Bible, the old Bible before changes in late BC and early AD, other Ancient Literature and the scientific facts of creation/evolution.

Think about it and see how you would change the story, but please, you must not ignore any of the 4 3 sets of the information.

I hope you enjoy my attempt.

About the Author

Hi! Thanks so much for your interest in my books!

My principal interests are true stories of the unusual or of the previously Unknown or unexplained. I have occasionally also written some fiction.

I was born in Memphis Tennessee and grew up in the small town of Saltillo near Tupelo Mississippi.

After graduating from Mississippi State University as an aerospace engineer I moved to Orlando Florida and worked for Lockheed Martin for 24 years. I advanced from an aerospace engineer to a Vice President of the Company and President of the Tactical Weapons Systems Division in Orlando.

I then formed Parks-Jaggers Aerospace Company and sold it 4 years later.

I continued my education throughout my career with a MBA degree from Rollins College and with Post Graduate Studies in Astrophysics at UCLA; Laser Physics at the University of Michigan; Computer Science at the University of Florida; and

Finance and Accounting at the Wharton School, University of Pennsylvania.

After selling my aerospace company I formed Quest Studios, Quest Entertainment and Rosebud Entertainment to make films at Universal Studios. I produced 10 films, directed 7 films and wrote 5 films produced at Universal Studios.

I then formed UnknownTruths Publishing Company to publish true stories of the unusual or of the previously Unknown or unexplained. These include books about past events so unbelievable that most people have relegated them to "myths".

I have published 22 books as previously listed. 18 of these have also been converted to audio books. I have an additional 12 books in development including the following:

Aging is Preventable describes how our new knowledge of the human aging process and supplementation protocols can essentially stop aging.

End of Honor, Death of the Mafia is a true story about how the Mafia lost its honor when its members talked during the Rudy Giuliani trials.

Federal Rat describes the true story of the life and capers of a career criminal and how he manipulated the Federal Justice System to keep getting out of prison and returning to his life of crime.

Crystal Healing describes the science of (potentially) healing crystals.

Shakma, Filming a Crazed Baboon describes the frustrating experience of making the film Shakma at Universal Studios with a crazed baboon.

Eden Evolution addresses the question: how did mankind really get started; was there a Garden of Eden?

Sex in the Ancient Churches describes how the ancients recognized that sex and the sun produced life and how they used it in their rituals and places of worship.

Female Sex, Orgasm and Love describes the science of the female sex process and the hormones and physical events resulting in true love.

How to Make a Zombie describes the science of how to make a true zombie and describes actual instances.

Dam I Didn't Know That describes interesting tidbits that most people do not know but are important enough to know.

Alien Arrival, the First Visit is a novel about alien encounters through the ages, and today.

Serial Killings Planned is the story of 2 serial killers working together to create enduring reputations.

About
UnKnownTruths
Publishing Company

UnKnownTruths Publishing Company was formed to publish true stories of the unusual or of the previously Unknown or unexplained. These stories typically provide radically different views from those that have shaped the understandings of our natural world, our religions, our science, our history, and even the foundations of our civilizations.

The Company's stories also include stories of the very important anti-aging, life-extending medical breakthroughs; stem cell therapies; genetic therapies; cloning and other emerging findings that promise to change the very meaning of life.

The Company also publishes stories from the past that are so unbelievable that they are generally considered to be myths. The published stories provide the evidence for the truth.

The Company currently has an additional 12 books in development.

Made in the USA
San Bernardino, CA
08 January 2014

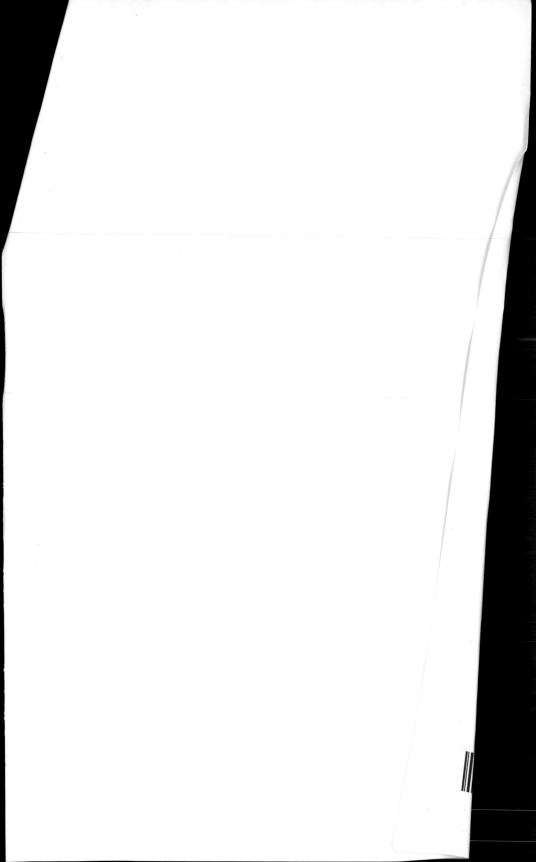